Were You There?

Diana L. Hayes

Art by Charles S. Ndege

Were You There?

Stations of the Cross

ORBIS BOOKS

Maryknoll, New York 10545

Second Printing, April 2004

The Catholic Foreign Mission Society of America (Maryknoll) recruits and trains people for overseas missionary service. Through Orbis Books, Maryknoll aims to foster the international dialogue that is essential to mission. The books published, however, reflect the opinions of their authors and are not meant to represent the official position of the society. To obtain more information about Maryknoll and Orbis Books, please visit our website at www.maryknoll.org.

Photographs of the Stations were taken by Fionnbarra O'Cuilleanáin, S.M.A.

Queries regarding rights and permissions should be addressed to:
Orbis Books, P.O. Box 308, Maryknoll, NY 10545-0308.

Published by Orbis Books, Maryknoll, NY 10545-0308
Manufactured in South Korea

Library of Congress Cataloging-in-Publication Data

Hayes, Diana L.
    Were you there? : Stations of the Cross / Diana L. Hayes ; art by
Charles S. Ndege.
      p.   cm.
    ISBN 1-57075-278-8 (pbk.)
    1. Stations of the cross Meditations. 2. Afro-American Catholics
Prayer-books and devotions – English.   I. Title.
BX2040.H38 1999
232.96 – dc21   99-30616

Contents

Introduction

The Lenten season is a critical time in the Christian liturgical calendar. It is a time to review the events of one's life, especially the preceding year, in order, hopefully, to learn from the acts — whether good, bad, or indifferent — that we have committed and that we have failed to commit. It is a time for remembering, as well, the Passion of our Lord and Savior Jesus Christ, in order to learn from him so that we might in our own life's journey better imitate his.

Jesus' life was a very brief one about which we know little. It is especially from the Gospel of Luke that we are able to learn some details of his birth and youth, his coming of age, his brief life of ministry, and his death and miraculous resurrection, a clear victory over death's grasp on all of us who have life.

What can we learn from this short life? What can we, as humans of every nation and tongue, learn from this man, Jesus, who walked the earth so many centuries ago? Is he no longer relevant, as many would have us believe, his message mired in a different time and a different context that speak to no one in the present day? I believe as we enter upon the twenty-first century, the third millennium of Christianity, that Jesus and his message are just as relevant today as they were long ago.

In this brief series of meditations on the Passion of Jesus on his last day of human life, I attempt to reveal the continued significance of the man and his message for me, an African American lay woman in the Roman Catholic Church, and for all others who call themselves Christian. Jesus was a human being like all of us who experienced, as we clearly read in the Gospels, both the promise and the pain of everyday human life. He was born into a poor carpenter's family, lived much of his life in an insignificant small village, Nazareth of Galilee, and preached his message of the coming of God's Kingdom for only a few short years. He was one of us, yet, in his divinity, he was unlike any of us.

For Jesus was truly the Son of God who, in his brief life, modeled how our lives should be led and by his death and resurrection freed us from death's stranglehold. He is the fulfillment of God's promise to all of creation that life does not end with death but is transformed into new life, a life not fully imaginable by us limited beings.

But Jesus is more, infinitely more. For many, but especially for my African American brothers and sisters, Jesus is the one who promised us not only liberation from the oppression of our fellow human beings but also salvation in the life to come.

It is, thus, fitting that this series of meditations should be illustrated by the beautiful and passionate work of Charles S. Ndege, a young Tanzanian artist commissioned to paint the Stations of the Cross on the walls of St. Joseph

Mukasa Church in Mwanza, Tanzania. The work took nine months, during which the artist lay or sat on scaffolding. The paintings depict typical scenes around the southern shores of Lake Victoria.

It is fitting that Jesus is depicted as a Black man, one of African descent. Just as he has been depicted over the centuries attired in the robes of the Jewish poor, Middle Eastern nobility, Renaissance princes, Flemish merchants, and English nobles, he is today rendered in a style and manner representative of the largest and fastest-growing Catholic community in the world, the church of Africa.

As Jesus was seen as Liberator, Savior, and Way-Maker for the oppressed slaves in the Americas and their descendants, so he is seen by their brothers and sisters separated by so many centuries and an ocean in their former homeland. He is Black, like them; he is poor, like them; he is humble but not subservient, like them; he is proud, like them; he is human, like them, but he is also so much more than they. His Passion resonates with the passion that has, far too often and for too long, been their lives, one of famine and disease; wars and violence; indifference from those with power and authority; illiteracy and poverty, a seemingly unconquerable poverty that stunts their growth, starves their minds, shortens their lives, and blights their spirits.

Yet, like Jesus, they believe in a God of love who brought them by their faith into a life of promise and who has never and will never fail them. This knowledge and understanding sustains them and has enabled them, whether African or of the African diaspora, not simply to survive but to thrive. They live their lives surrounded and immersed in faith in the one who came to set all captives free.

Jesus Is Condemned to Death

Station I

He stands, head bent, not in shame but in acceptance of his coming passion, knowing that his life and death will be vindicated in a way no one, certainly not this frightened Roman official sitting on his chief's stool busily washing his hands, could ever know or fully understand. Yet somehow centuries later, a people who are also held captive through no fault of their own, driven out in misty dawns with a curse and the lash, also know, in the deepest sense, what he felt that day. Standing patiently, mutely, looking straight ahead, hands bound, thorns digging cruelly into the tender flesh of his temples.

Way down yonder
By myself
And I couldn't hear
Nobody pray.

There stood the rooster, who had crowed to awaken the dawn and had also crowed confirmation that, at this moment, he was most truly alone, for all had fled, even Peter, the one he believed understood him best.

I've been 'buked an' I've been scorned,
I've been 'buked an' I've been scorned, children.
I've been 'buked an' I've been scorned,
I've been talked about sho's you' born.

Still a young man, Jesus looks toward the future, thinking what? Seeing, perhaps, a vision only he could see. Earlier that morning, he had prayed to his Father that this cup be taken from him, that this dreaded hour not approach. He was human and he feared with a human fear, but he was also the Son of God who rallied himself, almost before the words of prayer were even out of his mouth, changing them to acceptance, "Thy will, not mine, O Lord." He changed the words not from fear or weakness but from the strength of a faith that would carry him through.

Dere is trouble all over dis worl',
Dere is trouble all over dis worl', children.
Dere is trouble all over dis worl',
Dere is trouble all over dis worl'.

How prophetic these words sound today, in a world torn by wars, mindless hatred and violence, human greed and indifference. Today there are so many young men and women, of every race and ethnicity, who cry out with the same fear and anguish. They have the same doubts about their abilities to keep on and, yes, even the same anger. Why, O Lord? Why me? What must I do, what can I possibly do, to remove this bitter cup of hopelessness that is my life, to cast it away and begin a new life that is holy and wholly yours? For they did not ask for this life. They came as innocent children, born into a world where children are increasingly seen as a burden rather than a gift. Like Jesus, too many of them were born poor and outcast, misunderstood, ignored, from the wrong part of the city or country, with the wrong accent or skin color, hated, blamed for things they did or failed to do.

They were born into their blackness, their poverty, their isolation and alienation, into a world that is so threatened by those of us who are different, however that difference expresses itself. To be different is to be seen as dangerous, as a challenge to authority and the status quo. Often a mindless, numbing sameness is required to get along and move forward in life. Those who break this mold are branded as misfits to be quickly placed under control. So many young men and women were carried, innocent, in the wombs of women who bore them in pain and sorrow but loved them into life, hoping against hope that their lives would somehow be different, better. Others, however, did not even have that comfort. They were born to mothers rendered mindless by substance abuse, sick with HIV/AIDS, into families dysfunctional and abusive. They too are innocent but stamped guilty while yet in their mothers' wombs.

They are our sons and daughters, crying out for life against staggering odds: violence, drugs, disease, ignorance, hunger, and fear, the constant fear of all human beings of being unloved and unwanted.

> *Ain' gwine lay my 'ligion down,*
> *Ain' gwine lay my 'ligion down, children.*
> *Ain' gwine lay my 'ligion down,*
> *Ain' gwine lay my 'ligion down.*

Jesus died a martyr's death, a death not of glory and honor but the shameful death of a criminal, killed because he brought hope, killed because he, too, was different, hung out with the wrong crowd, didn't say what those in power wanted to hear. But he died a victorious death as well, not in vain, but in sacrifice for the lives of all of us. Jesus died as he lived, a man of faith who refused to lay down his religion, his faith in God, for anyone or anything. Then he rose from the dead to fulfill God's promise of salvation for all of humanity, rich and poor, of every race and nation, class and gender, age and tongue. Jesus brought life through his death. That young, robust man, standing there waiting for his cross to be placed on his shoulders, is not a victim but the victor. He is the one who paves the way for us all if we but follow him. We, too, must not lay our religion down. If we are to be like Jesus, in times of difficulty or doubt, we turn not away from the cross but toward it, claiming our faith from its victory and being sustained by that faith. We cannot do it alone, but just as Jesus was not alone, neither are we.

The path Jesus walked to his death was rock-strewn and dusty, full of potholes and ever-climbing, just as the paths of our own lives are. His path is our path. It is the path we all must walk at some point in our lives. But that walk must come because it is chosen as Jesus chose his, not because someone decides this child is not worthy of life; that this young woman is undeserving of health care; that this young man doesn't deserve a decent and full education; that this family is a burden to society and should be left to fend for itself. That is not the message of Jesus' life, death, and resurrection. No, that is a denial of faith. For Jesus told us to love God and our neighbor; one is empty without the other. Today, those whose lives are as empty as their stomachs, whose faith has deserted them because they never fully owned it, can reclaim their lives and their faith but only with each other's help and guidance. When we turn our backs on each other, we turn our backs on God. Like Peter, we deny Jesus once again.

God has promised us all life. Through Jesus' death and resurrection, life everlasting pours forth. Yet, somehow, we, God's creation, have gotten the message wrong. Too often we are like Pilate, refusing to judge but refusing also to take a stand, washing our hands, we believe, of any and all responsibility. But, in so doing, our very refusal, our continued denial of the humanity of those less fortunate than ourselves, those who are somehow different, condemns them to a needless and undeserved death even while they live. And we, also, are condemned for our failure of faith.

> *Way down yonder*
> *By myself*
> *And I couldn't hear*
> *Nobody pray.*

Jesus stands surrounded yet so alone. Who will pray for him? Who will pray for us? Who will stand up for him? Who will stand up for us? Who but us. And our God.

Jesus
Takes Up
His Cross

Station II

Were you there when they crucified my Lord?
Were you there when they crucified my Lord?
Oh, sometimes it causes me to tremble, tremble, tremble,
Were you there when they crucified my Lord?

We watch as Jesus lifts the heavy cross and puts it over his shoulder. It is a full cross, not just the crosspiece for the arms. The heavy tail drags, holding him back, causing him to stagger. He trembles under the weight of the cross and the lashes from the whip wielded so enthusiastically by one of the soldiers.

His eyes look ahead to the path he must take though he fears its end; it winds through the village upward to the top of Golgotha, the place of the skull. His hour has come; the cup has not passed him by. The journey begins.

Like Jesus, we, too, often dread the coming of an event or journey that we know will test us to our fullest extent. Our faith falters and trembles within us. We are afraid, unsure of our strength, of our ability to complete the journey that lies before us. At times like this, we often don't know where to turn or whom to turn to for assistance or guidance. We fear the answer we might receive or even the lack of an answer.

Jesus knew that his ending was only a beginning, for him and for all who believed in him and the one who sent him. This was his appointed hour and task, to bring all to believe in the one God, the God of Abraham and Isaac, of Moses and David, the God who created us all.

Too often today, we are unsure not only of our journey but also of its ending. We might start out in a spirit of joyful hope or quiet determination, seeking to get the task done and move on. We may struggle against it, refusing to move forward, feeling safe by remaining where we are. But the journey somehow begins, whether we are willing or not. It may be longer than we expect; it may require more of us than we think we are able to give or endure. We begin to give in to fear and discouragement, looking for an easy and quick way to go, seeking to find someone or something that will help us to make it through or do the job for or with us. We feel alone, even abandoned, afraid to go forward but equally fearful of turning back.

The Lord is my light and my salvation.

We turn to our friends, but perhaps they're too busy, caught up in their own journeys, overwhelmed by their own responsibilities, and they turn away, giving us a rushed answer that is unhelpful or a brusque refusal that deflates our spirits even more.

The Lord is my light and my salvation.

We turn to family — mother, father, sisters, brothers — but they too are unable or unwilling to help us. Perhaps they are absent from our lives, unable or unwilling to care for us because of their own weaknesses, their own fears and self-doubts. Perhaps they're present but are unwilling to risk once again, having helped us before only for us to turn away without a word of thanks or appreciation. Or perhaps they do offer help, but it is not in the form we want so we turn away, angry and frustrated, as do they.

The Lord is my light and my salvation.

To whom else can we turn? Strangers look at us and walk away shaking their heads. Like those around Jesus, others stand idly by, gossiping and chatting while we struggle to take up our own burdens, whether of poverty, unwed motherhood, drug or alcohol addiction, violence or abuse, greed or apathy, a life filled with too much to do and no time to do it, anger or shame. The list is endless, and the burden grows ever heavier as it seems to soak up our fears along with our faults.

Whom shall I fear?

There is only one to whom we can truly turn, only one who we know will never reject us no matter our sins, no matter our faults, only one who will answer us every time. That one is Jesus. For he too has been tempted; he too knows what it is like to stagger under the weight of a heavy burden. He knows what it is to love and be rejected, to trust and be abandoned, to watch friends and family turn away, shaking their heads in grief, frustration, confusion, or anger. He too sought aid and watched as his friends ran away in fear and trembling.

> *Whom shall I fear?*
> *Whom shall I fear?*
> *The Lord is the strength of my life.*
> *Whom shall I fear?*

Jesus is the one to whom we can turn when all hope is gone, when our strength has been poured out like water. Jesus answers the cries that come from the very depths of our souls, cries that we fear no one can possibly hear or understand. Jesus is our strength. By his death, he gives us life, a new life open to a new beginning, a journey companioned, a burden shared. Jesus restores our hope, rekindles our faith, shores up our faltering bodies, and guides us home.

> *The Lord is the strength of my life.*
> *Whom shall I fear?*

The journey, our lives, lies before us. Whom indeed shall we fear when Jesus has sent his Spirit to walk among us, sustaining, nurturing, carrying us if necessary, along our pilgrim way?

Jesus Falls the First Time

Station III

Jesus stumbles and falls. Perhaps a rock snagged his bare foot or a sudden dip in the path caused him to lose his balance. The weight of the wooden cross suddenly shifted, and he was on his hands and knees before the crowd of onlookers, unable to help himself. The soldiers shouted and lashed his back, as if he were a stubborn mule rather than their brother; he struggled to rise again.

Lord, help me to hold out.

Life is like that sometimes. You're on your way, busy with things and people, active and energized, feeling good about yourself and what you're doing. Then, suddenly and without warning, you find yourself laid low. Sick in spirit or in health. In the hospital, helpless to do anything and watching the days pass you by. Grieving the loss of a parent, spouse, child, or your former self. Death always comes too soon, leaving you feeling abandoned, with an emptiness within that seemingly can never be filled, a hole in the very core of your being. Your job, which you thought secure, is suddenly gone, stripped away. You're no longer needed or wanted there or anywhere else. You're told you're too old, that you lack the proper skills or knowledge. There are others who can do the task better or cheaper.

Lord, help me to hold out.

Those who were your friends, those who were always around you telling you how good you looked, how intelligent you were, how important you were to their lives, are suddenly gone as well. They've slipped away, not completely perhaps, but to the sidelines where they watch silently, shaking their heads, commenting to themselves and others.

You begin to realize that they weren't really your friends after all, just hangers-on, seeking to be seen with you, to share in your reflected glory. Now when you need them the most, on your hands and knees in the dirt with an unbearable weight crushing you, they're gone. Or they too are afraid of what might happen to them if they help you. Will "it" — whatever "it" is — rub off on them as well and affect their lives? They want to help but don't know how so they stand helplessly watching.

Lord, help me to hold out
Until my change comes.

Jesus knew the journey that he must take, the path climbing to a slow and painful death on the very cross he was now carrying. He glimpsed his Father's plan for him, knowing that his death was not an end but a beginning. Unlike Jesus, we don't usually know where our journey's end will be or what form it will take. We are usually caught unprepared, still struggling upward, searching for the way to go forward. Yet in our humanity, we are much the same. For Jesus, the way was still difficult, the burden much heavier than he had expected. As he knelt in the dirt, sweat and blood mingling as they poured down his face, feeling the thorns digging into his temples and the whip on his back, surely he prayed to the One who had sent him, asking for help, asking for the strength to go on, asking for endurance until his change, from death to resurrected life, would come.

My way may not be easy,
You did not say it would be.
But if it gets dark,
I can't see my way,
You told me to put my trust in Thee.

So many of us today have no one in whom we can fully put our trust, not even ourselves. Either because of things we've done or said or failed to do or say, we feel abandoned, alone, afraid. As life seems to continue to pass us by, as the successes once won now trickle through our hands like so many grains of sand, we wonder if it was worth the price. We fear there is no hope, no future for us, no one who will help us regain the path.

Lent is a time of repentance, a time for remembering not those who may have failed or hurt us but those who we ourselves may have betrayed in however great or small a way. This is a time for grieving, yes, over the losses we have incurred, but also a time of preparation, of prayer and even fasting, for the renewal of spirit that God has promised us if we would but be open to its coming.

We need to look again at the priorities we have set in our lives. What is truly important and what can be cast aside? Perhaps these were the stumbling blocks that caused us to falter and fall. Were we too intent on gaining success at any price? Did we seek to have the biggest and fanciest car even though we knew we couldn't afford it? Are we pushing our children too hard and fast, giving them too little time to simply be children? Do we demand too much of others while giving little of ourselves? Perhaps, once successful, we turned our backs on those coming after us, assuring ourselves and the world that we made it on our own, that we owe nothing to anyone, forgetting the many who came before us and helped us along our way, smoothing the path, warning us of upcoming obstacles, holding our hand when we were frightened and carrying us when we were unable to walk on our own.

Perhaps it is one of those ancestors, those saints, our sheroes and heroes, who now stand invisibly in our way, calling our name, trying to remind us of who and whose we are, hoping that this sudden and unexpected jarring fall may yet bring us to our senses. They call us to remember, remember that we are responsible, not only for our own lives, but for the lives of others, those with whom we interact and are connected in so many different ways as Jesus is connected to us all. We are indeed our brothers' and sisters' keepers, living, as all humans must do, in community, connected in so many ways with the lives and spirits of countless others.

As we fall on our knees, do we lift up our hands in supplication to God or in angry curses; do we reach out for the hand of another or for our wallets and purses to see if we can buy our way out? As we lie in the dust, are we humble or humiliated, emboldened or embarrassed, realizing what we had overlooked in our headlong rush to fame and fortune?

Lord, help me to hold out.

Jesus held out. Despite the loss of his friends, his followers, those who claimed they believed in him, he held out. Despite his weariness and pain, the heavy cross, the jeers and cries of those around him, he held out and he forgave them. He shouldered his cross once more and started forward again, knowing that though his physical body might be weak, his spirit, sustained by God, was strong enough to carry him through.

> *Lord, help me to hold out*
> *Until my change comes.*

We, too, can make it through, by recognizing and acknowledging our failures and our faults and by honestly seeking to overcome them. By lifting others upward as we ourselves climb, we gain strength; we do not lose it. By reaching out to others, affirming ourselves as Jesus did, we find, in our new solidarity, a strength and courage we did not know we had.

Jesus Meets His Mother

Station IV

This is my son. *My* son, with thorns piercing his tender flesh, the blood running down his face. He is so young, so handsome. He is my son, my child. I remember so clearly when the angel came to tell me I was to bear a child, a son who would be great among his people. I was overwhelmed. I knew not what to think or say. What would people think? I was betrothed but had never been with a man. How could this be? What would happen to me, to this child? But I knew I would say yes. I was called to this by God, and I trusted in God. So I said yes.

But is this what the angel meant by greatness? What could come of such pain, such indignity? This is my child. I would carry the cross for him as once I carried him, laughing and crying, on my back. What greatness can come at such a fearful price?

How long, how long, O Lord, must we mothers watch in silent agony as our children die before their time, weighed down by so many needless crosses not of their own making? Crosses of skin color, of poverty, of language, of sexual orientation, of fear, of lost hopes and discarded dreams. How long, O Lord, how long?

We cannot remain silent. These are our children, whether they came from our wombs or the wombs of others, helpless infants needing love and care. And now they die, at each other's hands, at the hands of those who were meant to care for them, the hands of indifference, of anger, of a corrosive hatred. These are our children, no matter how old or how young. They die. They die senselessly, needlessly, blindly, unknowing, without understanding why they must pay such a price. How long, O Lord, how long will this senseless slaughter continue?

Truly a sword is piercing my heart, the pain is so great. How could this be happening to my child, to my son? I remember when he was born. The night was so clear and the stars so bright they seemed to come right into that old stable where we had taken shelter. The warmth of the animals surrounded us as my labor began. I was so worried; this was my first and I had no one to help me. Elizabeth, my cousin, and the other women were back in Nazareth as I lay, racked with pain, in Bethlehem, the place of my husband's family. I had feared the ride on the donkey would cause my time to come, as the older women of the village had warned me. But we had no choice; we had to return to Bethlehem for the census.

And now my time had come. My little one was so eager to come forth I could barely control him. My husband tried to help but he was just a man, overwhelmed by the miracle of new life. The animals seemed to stare in wonder. Perhaps they knew what I was going through to bring forth this new life, a new life with so much promise. All mothers believe the same. How can they not? Each child is precious, an individual miracle, with a full life ahead. It was happening so quickly. He was born, my son, my little Jesus.

The Virgin Mary had a baby boy.
The Virgin Mary had a baby boy.
The Virgin Mary had a baby boy.
And they gave him the name of Jesus.

Jesus looks at me now as he has done so many times since he first looked at me in the stable. His big brown eyes seem to be full of the pain of the world. Who is this man, my child, my son? I hardly know him anymore, he has changed so. I was so proud of him as he gathered his followers and so many came forward to join him. He preached with such beauty and faith. This is my child, but truly he is God's as well. I thought I knew him, but every moment seems to reveal him in so many different ways.

The cross is so large. It seems to bear the weight of the world. Why is my son walking to his death dragging this heavy wooden cross? What has he done? He is so young and innocent. He has simply tried to do what God called him to do, to proclaim a message of peace and love for all of humankind. Why do so many see him and his message as a threat when it is a promise of unparalleled joy? He was not the first to speak God's word, but when he spoke, I saw entire crowds transformed, their faces, narrow with the pain of poverty and injustice, lighting up with a hope they had never before felt. All to whom he spoke, whom he touched, were transformed as I had been. His very presence spoke as much as his actions.

And now he walks to his death, but somehow I know, deep within myself, that his life will not end like that of others. There is more to come. His birth, witnessed by stable animals, peasants, and those three men from afar with their incredible gifts, his life, so brief, his death — all herald the coming glory of God. Truly I am blessed among all women to have been given the grace of being the mother of such a one, to have carried him within me for nine months, to have brought him forth in such pain and happiness. But for what? At times, his actions have brought me such fear, such pain. What is to become of my child? He is so young to die such a painful death. But I look at him and see his strength and resolve, and I am calmed. I fear for him because I am his mother but, like all mothers, I must let him go. His journey began with me, but now we come to a parting of our ways. His destiny calls him, and he walks on bent under that cross of wood. I send him on his way with a mother's blessing, with my love to sustain him, for it is all I have to give.

> *He come from the Kingdom.*
> *He come from the glorious Kingdom!*

Jesus was a strong man, a man sent to carry the burdens of the world upon his shoulders, transforming them into the joys of salvation. Where are the strong men of today? Where are our sons and their fathers? So many are bowed down and beaten or fighting the wrong enemies, or each other, rather than the poverty, hatred, and ignorance that keeps them trapped in meaningless lives of little hope.

Where are our strong young men, young men like Jesus, who stepped forward to fight the good fight, not just for themselves but for all who are wrongly used, imprisoned, struck down in the fullness of life? Where are our men of God like Martin, Malcolm, and Medgar, who walked this earth such a short time ago?

Their mothers seek them. Their children wait for them, with empty bellies and even emptier hearts. What has happened to our young men that has caused them to give up, succumbing to the temptations of this world, giving up their very souls little by little by little until there's nothing left to give?

Our faith no longer sustains them. The churches are empty, except for the old and the very young. The children are in the streets, filled with anger at the betrayal of the promise given to them at birth, the promise of a future filled with possibilities. They are burdened with new crosses that imprison rather than free them, crosses of crack cocaine, HIV/AIDS, death at the hands of strangers and of friends, children whom they have no time for or interest in, jobs that provide money to sustain them but give no joy, lives of emptiness but crammed with busyness.

We must reclaim these, our wayward children. We must gather them to ourselves and listen to their fears and their pain. We must meet them, as Mary did, on their painful journeys and attempt, through word and touch, to help them to see that they are not alone. We, their mothers, are with them; we will not abandon them, and neither will Jesus because he knows their sorrow and is acquainted with their grief. He is one of us and walks with us regardless of who we are and what we have done or failed to do. We wring our hands, feeling the pain of our young men as they wander like ghosts in a nightmare, but we also turn and walk alongside them, letting them know by our presence that they have not been and will not be abandoned. We are their mothers and we are not ashamed of their condition. We are their mothers and they are still our children. We must reclaim them for they too come from the kingdom, that glorious kingdom of God.

Simon Helps Jesus Carry His Cross

Station V

The blows of the whip keep falling as Jesus struggles to carry his cross up the ever steeper hill. How will he manage? Is there no one willing and able to lend a hand?

So often we speak in loud and boastful voices of what we would do if "such and such" a person would dare say or do something to us. But when that moment finally comes, our courage fails us, our hearts falter, we stutter and stumble over our words and, as soon as possible, take to our heels in desperate, fearful flight. So little has changed from the past.

At first, no one is willing to help Jesus bear his cross. Those following along, talking loudly, quickly flee. What do they have to fear? They have not been condemned to death. Yet, somehow they fear that they will be tainted by contact with this man Jesus whom they had, just a few days earlier, welcomed into the gates of their city with loud hosannas and waving palms. But even his disciples have abandoned him. Why should they risk what even those who believed in him will not risk?

So too today we are often quick to hold up those with new ideas who bring life and light into our lives. We see them as prophets, worthy of honor and praise. But at the first sign of trouble, when the first questions arise, how quickly we abandon the person or the plan and join in the attack. Little thought is given to the fact that they have risked their lives and futures for the benefit of others, including ourselves. We see only that they appear to have failed.

But one man, a Cyrenean named Simon who was coming in from the fields, stepped forward when the call went out for someone to help our weakening Savior. Simon stepped forth into history, taking up the tail of the cross, freeing Jesus of the dragging weight and earning salvation for himself.

Too often, as nay-sayers and doubters, we tend to be a dragging weight on someone else's hopes or dreams. Rather than giving them courage, rather than offering sound advice and assistance, we hang like leaden weights pulling them down. "No one has ever done it that way before. We've always done it this way. Why should we change? Someone else has always been in charge of this program or that event. You're too young to do it. You must think you're better than everyone else. It won't work, no one will support it, it's too different."

Where is our Simon of Cyrene who steps forward, fearfully yes, but no less courageously, and offers a helping hand? Such a simple gesture yet such a profound one, for by his actions he has freed himself while others flee.

Today, we continue to flee, turning our backs on those less fortunate than ourselves, those who may be different for whatever reason, those seeking to bring about change. We ignore their outstretched hands, their pleas for recognition and assistance, their need to be acknowledged and welcomed. We turn away, too busy, too full of our own lives, never realizing that in so doing we are turning away from God, condemning ourselves by our own selfishness and fear.

It is impossible in today's world for anyone to survive, let alone move forward, without some form of assistance from others. The problem is that to seek some forms of assistance is considered blameworthy. Yet, no one enters, lives, or leaves this life without someone else's intervention. That intervention can come in myriad ways great and small: an opened door, a word of welcome, wise counsel, a smile of recognition, a job offer, a meal, education or training in a particular field, transportation, books and paper and pens, clothing, a bed to sleep in, a place to wash up and rest, guidance, love, nurturing. The list is endless but the reward everlasting.

Veronica Wipes the Face of Jesus

Station VI

Beautiful, also, are the souls of my Black sisters.

— LANGSTON HUGHES

Black women have carried a double and oftentimes triple burden in this world, for they are Black, female, and too often poor in a world that disparages all three. Bowed down by ignorance, usually willful, and misunderstanding, they have, far too often, been required to carry the weight of the world on their weary shoulders.

Since the beginning of time, they have, as women, been blamed for the entry of evil into the world. The stereotypes that plague their every step — of overbearing matriarch, emasculating wife, and oversexed seductress — have followed them like a curse from generation to generation. Yet, somehow, they persevere.

> *I heard my mother say,*
> *I heard my mother say,*
> *I heard my mother say,*
> *Give me Jesus.*

In the face of seemingly insurmountable odds, they are able to keep their faith alive as they attempt — despite rejection and the loss of husbands, brothers, fathers, and sons — to nurture that faith and pass it along to those of their own time and those coming after them. They forge a chain of faith that passes down through the centuries, over rivers, valleys, and oceans.

Give me Jesus,
Give me Jesus,
You may have all this world,
Give me Jesus.

They stand firm, refusing to back down in the face of danger, assaults against themselves and, more importantly, against theirs, to encounter their child, their son, Jesus. Their hearts cry out at the pain they see furrowing his forehead, and one, Veronica, attempts to wipe it away with a piece of cloth. The soldiers are caught off guard and don't know how to respond; looks of consternation cross their faces. But Jesus, still being helped by Simon, pauses, looks at them, and blesses their faith and kindness. They too have gained salvation because they did not hesitate to comfort the Comforter in his time of need.

Veronica, unaware, receives a further blessing: the image of Jesus' face on her cloth as a sign of her faithfulness. So many women today remain unknown, faceless and forgotten, despite the courageous and countless acts of mercy they have performed down through the years. The unknown Black slave woman who knew the alphabet and a little bit of reading, knowledge that could have led to her death if discovered, who held classes at night after a hard day in the fields and taught class after class. Many took their new knowledge, forged passes, and fled, but she stayed behind, providing a way to the future. The women who sewed quilts, today seen as valuable pieces of folk art but then only as scraps sewn together to keep warm. The pattern on these quilts also provided guidance regarding the path to the North and freedom.

Dark midnight was my cry,
Dark midnight was my cry,
Dark midnight was my cry,
Give me Jesus.

There were women then of strength and an enduring courage, and those women still exist today, countless numbers of women who serve, unnamed and unknown, in homes, hot kitchens, shelters, hospices, schools, and churches, cooking, sewing, and cleaning, teaching and preaching a way out of no way into God's graced freedom.

Give me Jesus,
Give me Jesus,
You may have all of this world,
Give me Jesus.

Veronica and the women with her boldly walked up to Jesus, ignoring the soldiers and their weapons, and offered him aid. They prayed for him, giving him strength, their strength, to continue his journey, as mothers have prayed for their children for countless generations. Today other women walk with their children, of every nation and tongue, with their sons, in jail, in school, or in corporate or political office, with their daughters, college-bound or pregnant at too young an age. They walk because they must, because they love, because they care. They reveal the inner strength of women. They reveal the courage of women. They reveal the faith of women.

Oh, when I come to die,
Oh, when I come to die,
Oh, when I come to die,
Give me Jesus.

Give me Jesus,
Give me Jesus,
You may have all of this world,
Give me Jesus.

Jesus Falls the Second Time

Station VII

I cannot stand, the weight grows heavier and heavier. This does not feel like an ordinary wooden cross; it is so heavy and digs so painfully into my shoulder. I am so tired. The cross rubs the whip wounds on my back; they burn like fire as my sweat runs into the open cuts.

> *Sweet little Jesus boy,*
> *They made you be born in a manger.*
> *Sweet little holy child,*
> *Didn't know who you was.*

Where has everyone gone, my friends, the crowds that followed me everywhere and pushed against me so at times I could not move? They refused to leave me then, wanting to hear everything I said, leaving me little time to rest. They were so hungry, both physically and spiritually! I tried to feed them as best I could, but where are they now? They give me plenty of room now, standing back, their heads downcast, their looks fearful, as they watch me from the corners of their eyes.

Where are Peter and John, the seventy and the twelve? The cock crowed and I was denied. They ran away, leaving me to make the last part of my journey alone. They no longer crowd my steps, asking to sit on my right and on my left. I am alone, weighted down on every side. Alone.

> *Didn't know you came to save us, Lord.*
> *To take our sins away,*

Our eyes was blind,
We couldn't see.
We didn't know who you was.

How abandoned and alone Jesus must have felt as he walked the long, hot, and dusty path leading to the place of his crucifixion. How exhausted, drained physically and emotionally, sustained only by faith that he was doing the will of his Father. This was his cup that he had to take and drink, whether bitter or sweet.

His mother was in the crowd. He could feel her presence and that of the other women who had stood by him for so long, providing food and clothing to help him in his ministry. Their presence certainly gave him strength even though he knew they did not fully understand why he had to go through this final agony.

In the valley, on my knees, with my burden . . .
And I couldn't hear nobody pray.

If only someone would say a simple word of encouragement, would reach out a hand of comfort. But they are afraid, even, it seems, ashamed. They look away, scandalized that this man who seemed so powerful was now on his hands and knees in the dirt. They laugh and jeer, telling him to save himself. "I sure am glad that's not my son. Just look at him. I knew he'd come to no good with all that preachin' and healin'. Isn't he the one who started that fight in the Temple? Why, he's nothing but a carpenter's son, acting as if he were a great teacher. Well, he got what was comin' to him."

The worl' treat you mean, Lord,
Treat me mean too,
But that's how things is down here
Because we didn't know who you is.

How quickly we forget those who opened themselves to us, revealing their weaknesses and our own, those who lent us a hand when we were down and out with nowhere to go. How easy it is to walk away, secretly glad and relieved that it is not you or one of yours, hoping no one saw you in the crowd eagerly reaching out to be healed or fed.

How quickly we forget how our hearts beat faster and our breathing quickened when we were told that life did not have to be like this. That better times are coming. That it is wrong for us to be mistreated, misunderstood, miseducated, used, and abused, but now freedom is coming. The day of Jubilee.

We didn't really listen to the other part: that freedom would come only if we worked for it together as a community of faith; that better times were indeed right around the corner if we would set aside petty differences of race, language, gender, and class and simply "walk together, children" and not get weary.

You done told us how;
We's a tryin'.
Masta, you done showed us how,
Even when you's dying'.

At the first sign of trouble, at the first sign of difficulty, we flee, forgetting promises of solidarity, forgetting that "all things come together for those who wait upon the Lord." We grow faint-hearted and weary of the struggle. Now we're lost. We feel abandoned. He should have known better, we think, forgetting how we applauded and cheered his words and actions. So easily and quickly we turn our backs on those who seek only to help us, fearing that their behavior will be too disruptive. Complacency is much simpler and less wearying. Sometimes it seems we believe that the hell we know is better than the heaven we might achieve because it requires us to do something, to change our ways, to make an effort, to "let go and let God" take over our lives. But the promise is still held out, for Jesus did not give up. He fell, yes, but picked himself up and moved on. He had a commitment to see his journey through. And because of his commitment, because Jesus did not give up, we are able to see Jesus shining through the faces of all those with whom we come into contact. We live because Jesus died and yet lived. Glory! Alleluia!

> *Sweet little Jesus Boy,*
> *We didn't know who you was.*

Jesus falls for the second time. How many times will we allow the spirit of Jesus in our midst to fall before we realize that we, his brothers and sisters, must step forward to join him? We must cradle him, carry his cross and our own, not crosses of pain and fear, but crosses of hope and courage, crosses that we use to batter down the gates of injustice and ignorance and hatred that keep us trapped. With our crosses, we can truly transform the world, but we must first be transformed ourselves.

Jesus Meets the Women of Jerusalem

Station VIII

They were women then
My mama's generation
Husky of voice — stout of step
With fists as well as hands
How they battered down doors...

— ALICE WALKER

The women of Jerusalem gathered by the side of the path they knew Jesus would take. They greeted him with cries of pain and love. The one whom they loved was being taken from them. They stood in the path, kneeled in the dirt, and stormed the heavens with their pain-filled wailing.

Jesus, his brow streaming with blood and salty sweat, his robe soggy with the same awful mix, hears them and recovers his strength to stand. He looks at the women who had followed him, who had believed in him and continued to do so, and he is overcome.

The soldiers are dumbstruck. They know not how to counter these women, their women, and mothers, sisters, and daughters kneeling in the dust with their crying children at their feet and praising, through their tears, this man whom they were taking to his death. Why are they showing him such respect? He is no better than a common slave or thief, to be hung between two other thieves, the worst death possible. Who was this man whom many had condemned and yet so many others had exalted?

The women knew the truth of him. They understood the significance of his life and death. They cried but they also rejoiced that they were able to see him, to strengthen him on his way. They knew him as he knew them.

They knew what Jesus told them, that the future was bleak and their lives and their children's lives would be as nothing to those who were capable of killing such a man.

Daughters of Jerusalem, do not weep for me; weep instead for yourselves and for your children, for indeed, the days are coming when people will say, "Blessed are the barren, the wombs that never bore and the breasts that never nursed." (Luke 23:28–29)

Harsh words indeed from one about to die, but in their hearts they knew the truth of his words. And many lived to see them come to pass with the destruction of the Temple and the scattering of their people.

Today we too can see the truth of Jesus' words. Look at our cities, our schools, our streets and the devastation and despair present there. Look also at our children. They are old before their time, forced to take on duties and responsibilities beyond their years. They are confronted with choices no one should have, child or adult. Should they become gang members, to find the family that no longer exists at home and to provide themselves with protection? Should they try drugs, which are available on every street corner, even in their schoolyards, or should they listen to their parents and other adults who warn them of the dangers while they themselves are smoking and drinking themselves to death?

It is not easy being a child today. Children look for certitude, for guidance from the adults around them, but too often they find themselves victims instead. We fill our lives with so many important things that we have no time for life, for the children, for their hopes and dreams. They grow bitter and angry, foul-mouthed and profane. They laugh off school as a waste of time or pursue an education with a single-mindedness that leaves no room for the simple pleasures of life. They have too many role models who refuse to act as such and too few who are capable of helping them to make the right decisions in their lives.

Our children, bereft of all that sustains and nurtures life, too often find themselves abandoned and alone. And the women, the mothers, cry. They cry for Jesus; they cry for themselves; they cry for their children and the loss of hope.

Women bear the future in their wombs. They are the bearers of culture, the tellers of stories, the weavers of dreams. They too have fallen victim, like so many men, to the easy way out, the quick climb up the ladder of success, abandoning all they believed in along the way, or the even quicker fall into substance abuse and prostitution for the quick release from pain, fear, and frustration.

Jesus walks on to his destiny knowing that it will end in glory, the salvation of us all. We walk on as well, some quickly and surely, others stumbling and faltering, all seeking the Way, the true path of life.

Amazing grace,
How sweet the sound
That saved a wretch like me.
I once was lost
But now am found,
Was blind but now I see.

Open your eyes. See the world around us, crumbling into chaos. Draw strength from the one who gave his life so that all might live. And live!

Jesus Falls the Third Time

Station IX

The path is never-ending. The sweat beads and drips down his face, mixed with the blood from his "crown," blinding his eyes, making it harder to see the rocks and pebbles, the dips and bumps under his aching feet. The soldiers lash his back unmercifully, uncaring that the day is hot, the sun blinding, the cross unbearably heavy to a man already weakened from fasting and blood loss. If anything, they blame him for having to be out in the sun themselves rather than relaxing back at the barracks.

The people watch and whisper, hiding their faces in shame and embarrassment for him, yet no one lends a hand except the faithful Simon, still holding the tail of the cross. The weight of the cross seems to grow heavier and heavier, as Jesus' strength flows out of him like water.

Water! Oh, for a drink of cool, cool water. One of the soldiers has carried a bucket from which he and the others drank, but none was offered to Jesus. Trying to swallow through a mouth parched from gasping for air, Jesus stumbles and falls for the third time.

Jesus' way is our way. His burden is our burden. For centuries, persons of African descent toiled in the hot, burning sun from "can see" to "can't see." With few breaks for water or food, the women carried their children on their backs or tucked them into a hollow or under a bush, wherever they could find a bit of shade. And they wondered about the God the master kept telling them about. This God-man, Jesus, seemed to have more in common with them than with the master. And didn't the Book say he died so that all could be free? Isn't that what he said himself when he first preached and nearly was killed for saying he'd "come to set the captives free"? If all that's true, shouldn't it mean that we should be free too? Not somewhere down the road when we die, but right here and right now? Weren't they God's children too despite what Master and Missus said?

They knew of a wonder-working God who had proclaimed liberation for all of God's creation. They knew they were a part of God's creation. They understood how Jesus felt as he toiled along that seemingly endless, dusty trail toward his death. They understood because they had experienced hard labor under a burning sun, the indifference of the overseer to their thirst and hunger, the blows and lashes rained down upon them if they slowed for even a second to stand up and stretch their aching backs, to wipe the sweat from their eyes.

They understood his pain, his fear, his weariness. Yet they were able to sing songs of faith that strengthened them on their pilgrim journey, songs of hope that buoyed them up and let their spirits rise above the dusty, burning fields.

> *There is a balm in Gilead*
> *To make the wounded whole.*
> *There is a balm in Gilead*
> *To heal the sin-sick soul.*

Today we also know that the struggle is ongoing. African Americans were born of a struggle to survive and thrive against the blows of slavery, Jim Crow segregation, and racism in the United States. That we have not only survived but have been able to move ahead is a testimony to the faith of those who came before us and kindled the fire of resistance within us. But today that flame is in danger of going out, both from the threats of others and from the apathy of ourselves. Our children are bowed down with more crosses than they can bear: illiteracy, poverty, sexism, racism, classism, homophobia, materialism, individualism, consumerism, on and on and on.

Unlike Jesus and even their ancestors, they are unable to look ahead to a different tomorrow, one bright with hope. They stumble along, eyes on the ground, drained of strength, initiative, hope, and courage. They have lost their way because we, too often, have failed to show it to them. The path has become hidden and lost, overgrown and unused. They do not know the life-giving and life-affirming faith that was sung about in the past because no one has attempted to teach them the words.

> *If you cannot sing like angels,*
> *If you cannot preach like Paul,*
> *You can tell the love of Jesus,*
> *And say he died for all.*

For too many of our children today, there is no balm in Gilead; there is no one and nothing to heal their sin-sick souls. They don't know the answers and have forgotten the questions. We must sing them into life again, sharing the stories, the songs, the prayers of our foreparents that will heal the wounds that threaten to destroy them. It is our responsibility to rekindle that flame within them, to tell them the "old, old stories" and sing to them the songs of old as well. But the stories must be told and the songs sung in new ways that they can understand, in rhythms that penetrate their minds, hearts, and souls, and in images that reflect their own rich beauty.

Jesus Is Stripped of His Garments

Station X

The final hours are now approaching. What were the thoughts of those who removed the clothing of this man, Jesus? They really knew very little about him. He did not fight nor did he cry out his innocence as the others did. Throughout his trial and weary, burdened journey, he said few words. I'm sure they wondered, "Who is this man?" Even as they made sport of him earlier, crowning him with thorns and kneeling mockingly in his presence, did some of them wonder, "Is he really the one others claim that he is?" He shows no anger nor fear; yet he is not passive. He stands, walks, stumbles, falls, but continues to move forward to his death as if there was a greater purpose to his effort than death. As they took his clothes and later gambled for their share of the blood- and sweat-stained garments, did they wonder at their own fate?

Oh, to have the strength of Jesus, not a physical strength, but a spiritual strength so focused on the final goal that little else seems to matter. He felt the pain of the whip; he felt the strength ebbing from his body; he wondered at all that was happening to him, yet he persevered.

We've come this far by faith.

Jesus' faith in himself and his Father sustained and nurtured him, enabling him to place one trembling, weary foot before the other as the road kept climbing.

Leaning on the Lord.

The Lord God, creator of all, was with him from his birth and at every step of his journey toward death on a wooden cross, the death of a common criminal.

Trusting in his holy word.

If only we, as a people, as a nation of immigrants both willing and unwilling, could somehow return to that earlier faith of our forefathers and foremothers. Theirs was a faith in the unseen and the unwitnessed, a faith that helped them to live and grow stronger regardless of the obstacles in their path, the denial of their faith by others, the stripping away of their human dignity.

God's never failed me yet!

If we could simply recall how these others managed to come through the fiery furnace of life, refined, purified, and made whole, strengthened in the broken places, then surely we could begin to make a difference in our own lives and the lives of those around us. There is so much that is contrary to God's will present in today's world. The mark of the Evil One seems to be everywhere, leaving its stain on everything we love and cherish. No nation or people has totally escaped that taint. We quarrel and kill each other over ancient grievances, long forgotten by most until someone dredges them up for their own self-righteous purposes. We are separated by things we cannot control, such as the color of our skin and the texture of our hair, attempting to prove the superiority of one over the other. We hunger and thirst, not for the Word of God, but for the products of a fallen humanity — wealth, property, success, fame, and power — all distractions that will not bring us closer to the Kingdom of God but drag us further away. We have torn apart the Body of Christ, leaving it a bleeding ruin, its parts at war with each other rather than working together in harmony. By our own acts and omissions, our failure to act as brothers and sisters to each other, we have turned our backs on those who need us the most.

> *Just the other day*
> *I heard someone say*
> *He didn't believe in God's word;*
> *But I can truly say*
> *That God has made a way*
> *And he's never failed me yet.*

God's never failed me yet. As we continue on our journey home to that same God, a God who loved us into being and then gave us the freedom to choose, to choose even against God, we need to ask ourselves how our ancestors survived — slave and free, rich and poor, of many colors but all of the same race, that of humanity. What was the secret that kept them afloat and why does it now escape us? Why did they not pass it down to us as it must have been passed down to them and those before them? Or is it that we did not listen, that we shrugged aside their efforts to tell us, seeing their stories as rambling and meaningless? As we look at ourselves, as we look deeply into the core of our being, are we surprised by the emptiness that we discover? When we look at our children, do we wonder that they know nothing of grace, of human dignity, of pride in self and in one's efforts, of civility, of common decency and shared responsibility? How can they learn what has not been taught or modeled by their elders?

> *We've come this far by faith*
> *Leaning on the Lord.*

To lean on the Lord is to recognize that as fallen humanity it is impossible for us to save ourselves. It is to recognize the limitations of human flesh and will and to acknowledge our need for God's gracious guidance. It is to call upon the Lord, in faith, knowing that our call will be answered, perhaps not in the time we might desire but it will be answered. This insight, however, can come to us only when we have truly "let go and let God" in trusting love, when we have given up our struggle to control everything and everyone around us and allow God to enter our lives, when we have become like little children once again and reach out for God's hand to help us along our way.

> *Don't be discouraged*
> *When trouble's in your life,*
> *He'll bear your burdens*
> *And move all misery and strife.*

Those who have gone on before us knew they had to put their hands in the hand of God. And when they did, they knew everything would be all right. When Jesus came to his final hour, he put all his trust in his Father and was able to stand, exhausted yet unmoved, as his clothes, his only material possessions, were stripped from him and gambled away. He knew what we must know once more, that God would not fail him.

Jesus Is Nailed to the Cross

Station XI

Were you there when they nailed him to the tree?
Were you there when they nailed him to the tree?
Oh, sometimes it causes me to tremble, tremble, tremble.
Were you there when they nailed him to the tree?

As the nails pierce his skin, Jesus looks upward, eyes wide open, to the heavens from where he knows his strength and hope come. He is so weary, after much loss of blood and the heavy weight of the cross. Now the cross must carry him, bear his weight upward into the afternoon sky. It is almost at an end.

He has not turned away. He has not flinched from the cup that was his to drink but has drunk deeply and drained it completely. Soon he will be free of all life's burdens, free to return to his home, to his Father who sent him forth so many years ago.

So often when a new challenge enters our lives, when we are called upon to do something we've never tried before, when we are required to stretch and grow in ways we've never done before, we hesitate and falter. Our initial reaction is to say no, I can't do it. I've never done anything like this before. I'm not prepared. I'm comfortable where I am and with what I'm doing. Call on someone else, I'm not quite ready yet.

Sinner, please don't let this harvest pass.
Sinner, please don't let this harvest pass.

Sinner, please don't let this harvest pass.
And die and lose your soul at last.

We often don't realize that to live is to grow, not to take the soft and easy way but to tackle the more challenging path even though it may, at first sight, appear rock-strewn, dirty, twisting, and narrow, and uphill all the way. We'd rather take another path, or else we believe we should be allowed to ride in style past all of those other struggling pilgrims. We want the express route.

But a life of faith is neither that easy nor that simple. If we truly want to be followers of Jesus the Christ, the Risen Lord, then we must be willing to pay the price he paid, to put our very lives at risk. We risk the disapproval of friends and colleagues. We risk discomfort and even actual pain, physical or emotional. But we risk because we know that risking strengthens us; risking prepares us for the tasks God will set before us if only we believe. We risk because that is the meaning of being a follower of Christ, who risked all so that we might have life in its fullness.

I know that my Redeemer lives,
I know that my Redeemer lives,
I know that my Redeemer lives.
Sinner, please don't let this harvest pass.

My Redeemer lives. He who died on the cross for me and for you now lives on high, seated at the right hand of our creator. We have been promised the same reward for our steadfastness in our faith as Jesus, a glorious resurrection and new life among the blessed. The grace to believe has been given us; the choice is now ours to step forward into a new life or to hang back in fear of the consequences.

The way is indeed difficult, but not because God willed it so. It has become a tortuous path because of our own actions and the failure of humanity toward our fellow human beings. We are the ones who place the obstacles in our path, finding bigger and bigger boulders and potholes through our fear, our indecision, our doubt, our anger, our sorrow, our greed. We hesitate, procrastinate, doubt, and mistrust those who are sent to us as messengers. We want to believe but are afraid of what others will think of us.

God does not will our suffering. Too often it is the result of the brokenness of our lives, our disconnectedness from God and from each other. We find ourselves too busy to pray, too busy to love, too busy to learn of and from each other.

Instead, we fear each other's differences. We turn our backs and walk away, claiming regret at our inability to change, yet failing to act against those who willfully seek to perpetuate the brokenness of our lives and world.

Where is our God? Is he found in the coffee bars, the gyms and fitness centers, the churches, the schools? Where is he to be found today? Where is our hope when we are at our lowest, when we have been pressed on every side and feel about to crack from the pain of loss, of despair, of indifference and hatred? Where is our Redeemer?

Sinner, oh, see the cruel tree.
Sinner, oh, see the cruel tree.
Sinner, oh, see the cruel tree.
Where Christ died for you and me.

Christ did indeed die for you and me. Jesus suffered on the cross and died so that we might have life everlasting, not broken lives of pain and violence, not a life of perpetual toil and struggle, but a life secure in the knowledge that no one has to endure such a death again. Yet so many have endured such deaths and continue to do so, hung from trees and burned in ovens, slaughtered because of their faith or their ethnicity. So many innocent have continued to die because we are afraid to stand up and proclaim the injustice of what we, all God's creatures, are doing to each other.

What have we learned from any of this needless slaughter? What have we learned from the death of this humble man who was so much like us and yet so much more? Have we learned nothing?

My God is a mighty man of war,
My God is a mighty man of war,
My God is a mighty man of war.
Sinner, please don't let this harvest pass.

We sing, even as Christians, of war in so many ways, with images that are war-like and violent. Is this why Jesus endured violence to his own body, a violence that continues, so that we might inflict violence on our brothers and sisters? Surely not. His battle is not one for power, land, or money, but a war of justice, a battle for righteousness, a war to end the suffering in all of its many forms. Our God has indeed fought our battles, but more importantly, our God is a God of peace, one who brings liberation to those wrongly oppressed, justice to those ill-used and abused and blessed, blessed peace to those who are weary of the constant wars we wage among ourselves and even within ourselves. If we would but heed his call: "Come unto me, all ye that are heavily laden and I will give you rest. For my yoke is easy and my burden is light."

> *Were you there when they nailed him to the cross?*
> *Were you there when they nailed him to the cross?*

The road is indeed dusty, rocky, and exhausting, seemingly endless and always uphill because we have made it so, building it and rebuilding it with fear, self-doubt, jealousy, envy, anger, hatred, greed for power, and the denial of love. Jesus died so that we might have life in abundance, untainted by sin and its senseless violence. We have, however, in our blindness, in our weakness and faint-heartedness, too often chosen death instead of life, turning paradise into hell.

> *Sometimes it causes me to tremble, tremble, tremble.*

Our God has not, our God will not abandon us despite ourselves and our actions. God calls and calls and calls yet again, holding out a hand that will ease the pain and suffering. He continues to shower us with the grace to respond to that call.

Hush, hush, somebody's calling my name.
Hush, hush, somebody's calling my name.
Hush, hush, somebody's calling my name.
Oh, my Lord, oh, my Lord, what shall I do?

Listen. Hear. And say yes.

Jesus Dies on the Cross

Station XII

Sometimes I feel like a motherless child,
Sometimes I feel like a motherless child,
Sometimes I feel like a motherless child,
A long way from home,
A long way from home.

Alone. Abandoned. Forsaken. No one to turn to, no one who cares. The most awful feeling for any human being is to feel completely alone, especially in the midst of suffering. How can anyone understand the anguish, physical, emotional, spiritual that I am going through right now? Is there no one who will even try, who will walk with me this sorrowful way?

Jesus dies on the cross. The physical pain is excruciating but the emotional anguish is even greater. Where are all of those who said they would follow him anywhere? Where are those who waved palms and danced with joy, singing "Hosanna!" when he entered Jerusalem just a few short days ago? Where are they now? They look on fearfully, afraid to say a word of comfort or support, afraid they too will be seized by the guards and suffer Jesus' fate.

Where are his faithful disciples who walked with him the dusty roads of Galilee, who argued over which one would have the honor of sitting on his right and left, positions now occupied by two thieves who die alongside him? They have abandoned him. Peter, the Rock, crumbled like wet sand

and denied him three times. The others simply watched as he was carried away by the soldiers. Others ran, one, in his haste, leaving his clothing behind, so quickly did he flee. Now they cower in an upper room behind a locked door, wondering what will become of them.

Only John remains, standing at his feet, and the women, his mother to whom he has given John as her new son, the two Marys. They have been stalwart and steadfast although they too fear what will come next. Their son, their beloved, their friend and teacher, is dying, stretched out on a wooden cross, cruelly executed in his innocence because of the fear and jealousy of others. What will happen now?

Jesus feels death approaching, life running out his side where the guards pierced him. As he weakens and slumps, it is even harder to get his breath. The pain is awful.

> *Sometimes I feel like a motherless child,*
> *A long way from home.*

All of his life had been for this moment, yet he still feels unprepared. He had simply tried to do the will of his Father, the will of God, as best he could, as we all attempt to do. And now the end approaches. His has been such a brief and selfless life. Born in poverty in a stable, raised in Nazareth, an insignificant Galilean village, he spent his life as a carpenter, with a few short years preaching the coming of God's Kingdom.

How familiar this must sound to many today. In towns and cities, rural areas and suburbs, throughout our nation, there are many like Jesus.

Children, born of hope, to young women, often barely out of childhood themselves, like Mary. They live lives of poverty and indifference, of wealth and neglect, learning how to raise themselves, to fend for themselves, wary of strangers and those who would call themselves friends, wondering what their future will bring or whether they have a future.

Some, still children, dream of bright futures, loving parents, fancy jobs and all that goes with them; others, old before their time, make meticulous plans for their funerals, for they know that they don't have a future, that their lives will soon be ended by an act of senseless violence and rage. They are children of all skin colors, of every race and ethnicity, who have no past to remember, no future to look forward to, and a present without promise.

Jesus in his dying agony cries out to his God in words each of these children would understand. "Father, O Father, why have you forsaken me?" Mother, what did I do to make you abandon me, to lose your love? Why am I all alone in this, my hour of greatest need? Where are those who said they would take care of me? Why was I born if they did not want me? What will happen to me now?

Where are the fathers of today? Too many are themselves dying, although their deaths take different forms. Some die the quick death of a gunshot, others the slower death of HIV/AIDS, others still the lingering death of the same hopelessness their children fear, too little education or the wrong skills, too old or ill. They too fear the future and try to run away from it by running away from family and responsibilities. Some don't even remember the brief encounter that brought a new life into the world.

Pass me not, oh gentle Savior,
Hear my humble cry,
While on others thou art calling,
Do not pass me by.

In the depths of our despair, we call out to God, as Jesus did, asking, praying to be remembered, asking to be loved, to be sheltered, to be cared for, seeking reassurance that we are wanted, that someone cares about our living and our dying. Where is our God in this time of critical need? Where are those supposedly trained to take care of the widow and the orphan, those damaged in mind and body and spirit? To whom can we turn?

There are so many hanging on crosses now, needlessly hanging. Some are on crosses of their own making, carved with torn and broken hands. Others are on crosses made by others who have appointed themselves to be in God's place.

True believer, true believer,
A long way from home.

We have all wandered far from home. So many of us have lost our way, forgetting how to return. We try to call upon God, but we've forgotten how. The words no longer come easily to our lips. The prayers, stories, songs are forgotten and those who tried to teach us are now themselves gone. They were the ones who paved the paths for us, but we turned away, seeking an easier or fancier way to travel, thinking their ways old-fashioned and out of date in today's fast-moving, hectic world.

The old ones were the true believers. If we would slow down our hectic pace, if we would pause in our overfilled days and listen, just listen, we might hear them calling us home, the mothers and fathers, grandmothers and grandfathers, the ancient ones, our ancestors, who knew all the paths to God.

While on others thou art calling,
Please don't pass me by.

Alone. Abandoned. Forsaken. Jesus dies on the cross. Children die in cross fires. Young adults die in too many ways to count as they fight to survive. Mothers smoke crack and fathers languish in jail. Others chase fruitless dreams thinking money will solve all of their problems.

It is God who is alone, who has been abandoned, who has been forsaken. We have walked away, turned our backs, turned to other gods, but they cannot sustain us.

Jesus overcame his fear, forgave those who had participated in his death, and died. Jesus will not abandon us if we turn to him, regardless of the words, the prayers we use. If we forget, he always remembers.

Jesus
Is Taken
Down from
the Cross

Station XIII

Honor, honor
Unto the dying Lamb!

The man Jesus has died. His friends ask that they be allowed to take his body down from the cross so that they may bury him. The Sabbath is coming and with it the celebration of the Passover. It would be a dishonor to leave his body hanging when he is already dead. The Paschal Lamb has been sacrificed; Jesus has atoned for the sins of all humankind with his death. It is now finished.

His limp body is slowly lowered into the waiting arms of his mother, who looks at her son through eyes cloudy with tears. "This is my son, my child, whom I bore in great labor and pain. And now he is dead. My son has gone before me to be with his Father in heaven. What will become of me now, a woman alone?"

There are too many women alone today whose husbands, the fathers of their children, and whose sons and daughters, the children of their wombs, have gone on before them. What will become of them now? How will they manage to raise their other children? How will they survive their old age with no one to care for them? We have gone outside the natural order of life: children should not die before those who gave them life.

Our world is out of sync; we know not where to turn as death and destruction surround us, in the foods we eat, the places we live, the very air we breathe. What will become of us all if we are unable to recognize each other's God-given humanity? Will we continue to crucify each other, forgetting that the sacrifice has already been made, our sins have been forgiven? Why do we continue to perpetuate the killing, allowing sin to enter once more into our lives and the lives of those we love? All of us are human; we are all born of parents who brought us into life, with hope or in fear, but believing that our lives would, should, be better than their own.

Why do we continue to sacrifice our own lives and those of others to senseless and needless death, whether the living death of being entrapped in dead-end jobs that make of our lives a never-ending cycle of despair or the actual death of senseless violence and unending warfare? When will we realize that the death of even one human being diminishes us all? We are indeed our brothers' and sisters' keepers, responsible for their hopes and dreams, agents of their despair, connected to them not just by blood but by our co-createdness by God.

> *King Jesus lit the candles by the waterside*
> *To see the little children running to be baptized.*
> *Honor, honor*
> *Unto the dying Lamb!*

There are too many of us hanging from crosses today, too many dying in pain and agony on crosses erected as a result of human inhumanity, of human indifference. Just as those who enabled the death of Jesus, not by any actual act on their part, but by their indifference, by their passivity, by their jealousy, by their fear of someone who didn't fit into their little boxes, so every day we crucify those around us, both known and unknown. They are the faceless poor, the poorly educated, the hungry and homeless, those abandoned on our streets, in our schools and churches, those left to fend for themselves because those who should care don't. We have hung them on the cross, a cross not of their own making, by denying them the right to a decent, full, and worthy life; by condemning them to early deaths in our ghettos and barrios, on our farms and in our tenements, in our skyscrapers and suburban split-levels.

Is anyone listening? Can we not hear their cries? They are the cries of a mother sobbing over the body of her son, pierced by knives or bullets of those who seek to prove their power or superiority over others by indiscriminate killing. They are the cries of a child weeping for his mother lost to him because of someone's drunken rage, by someone's failure to care. Can we not hear? Mary receives the limp body of her dead son. How heavy he is. Images flash through her mind: his smile, his eyes lighting up when he first saw her; his voice, first high and piping then gradually lowering so that she almost did not know this tall young man who had been a crying infant in her arms. And now he lies still and silent. Then she could cradle his entire body in her two hands, now his body is too long. She can't gather all of him up as once she could and rock him.

So many have died in countless wars that have resolved nothing. So many have lost arms and legs, have lost their very minds as a result of the violent weapons of destruction we have loosed upon the earth. When will it end? What does it mean that this man Jesus died almost two thousand years ago? There is no meaning if we continue to make war against each other. There is no meaning to Jesus' death if we continue to kill and be killed, to hurt and maim, to close our eyes to the harm being inflicted on those least able to defend themselves, the children, the old, the ill, women of every age and nation, the poor, the needy.

Can we not hear? Listen. Listen to the cries of the women mourning their lost ones; listen to the cries of the men seeking their wives and mothers, hunting the children lost to them; listen to the children alone and afraid, crying in the darkness of their fears.

Jesus died so that we might live. We deny his death when we turn our backs to the death on our streets, when we wash our hands of responsibility as Pilate attempted to do. But the blood cannot be washed away. We will not survive as a people until we recognize the humanity of all, until we acknowledge that we are all one in Christ Jesus, until we affirm that we are the caretakers of each others' souls. Skin color, ethnicity, gender, sexual orientation, economic status, none of these mean a thing. How do we dare to say we love God while hating those who are our neighbors? How do we dare?

Honor, honor
Unto the dying Lamb!

We owe honor to Jesus, Son of the living God, and to our neighbors, who are ourselves. We honor them because they, like us, are human; they, like us, struggle to live life one day at a time and sometimes can manage only one hour at a time. We honor them because they, like Jesus and like us, are made in the image and likeness of that same loving Creator who promised us all new life in him.

It is time for us to take down from their crosses all who have died so that they can lie in peace. It is time to heal the wounds of those still alive and help them down from their crosses of despair. It is time to chop up the wood of the crosses so wrongly erected and use them to light a fire that will warm the world, burn away all hatred and pain, and serve as a sign of our victory over death and all of its evils.

Honor, honor
Unto the dying Lamb!

Jesus Is Laid in the Tomb

Station XIV

Were you there when they laid him in the tomb?

I t is finished. The crowd begins to move away. The man Jesus is dead. He has been wrapped in cloth, just as he was wrapped at his birth in the cold stable, and carried to the tomb. There are no shepherds sent by angels, no wise men come to honor him. Just his mother and a few courageous friends. His mother, Mary, walks alongside as Jesus is carried to the tomb where he will be laid. Her head is bowed, her hands held together in prayer. "Thy will, not mine, O Lord," the words her son uttered in humble submission in the garden.

Were you there when they laid him in the tomb?

Now it is over. The dream has died with this gentle man of humble origins. He was a carpenter and a fisher of men and women who dared to preach God's love for the least among us, the poor, the widowed and orphaned, the women, those beaten down by despair and disease.

The women had remained faithful in the face of the threat of arrest and condemnation. They prayed, standing at his feet as he hung dying. They helped to bring him down from the cross and gave him to his mother to be cradled one last time in her arms. They wept with her and walked with him to his place of rest.

Had the dream died? Was this the end of it all? Jesus, the man, was dead.

His lifeless body lay in the tomb waiting for the stone to be rolled across the front, sealing him and the hopes of so many inside.

Were you there when they laid him in the tomb?

The events of that day were so incredible that many still could not believe what they had seen and heard. When this man died, the earth shuddered as if in labor, the sky suddenly grew as dark as night in the middle of the day. Even the soldiers, boldly gambling over his clothing, were shaken, their leader exclaiming the first words of Christian faith: "Surely, this man was the Son of God."

Oh, sometimes it causes me to tremble, tremble, tremble.

The earth trembled: the saints rose and walked the earth. The hearts of the hardest were opened. The veil of the temple was torn in two and darkness, a great darkness as if all of creation was in mourning, engulfed the sky.

This man, Jesus, in his few years on earth preaching the Good News of God, had an impact unlike any man before him. He had lived a life of poverty, working with his hands. His followers had been, for the most part, humble men and women — fishermen, tax collectors, prostitutes, the sick, the lepers, the poor, slaves. For them, his words opened up new possibilities in life, a life not of constant, endless, thankless drudgery, but a new life, one of plenty and peace, of a new freedom of mind, body, and spirit.

Were you there when they laid him in the tomb?

How could this be? It is now finished. Was it all a dream? The miraculous events of the past were forgotten and those to come not known as yet. As poor in death as in life, Jesus was laid in a tomb belonging to Joseph of Arimathea, a wealthy man who had earlier engaged Jesus in debate and found his life completely changed. He donated his own newly carved tomb, hewn out of the very rocks of the mountain where Jesus had been crucified.

How is it possible for life to go on after one you loved perhaps more than life itself is now dead? How do we keep from sinking into despair and hopeless grief? How do we maintain our faith, knowing that the one we loved no longer walks the earth alongside us? How? How?

We go on because we know the rest of the story. We know that Jesus' death is not the end, either of his life or of ours. His death is a new beginning, one unattainable before. By his death and glorious resurrection, death itself has been conquered and is no longer a threat to us.

Glory! Alleluia!

Jesus' death on the cross, his burial in the tomb, teaches us that death is not the end. After death comes a new life, one without pain or suffering, without fear or doubt, a life of joy that goes beyond all human understanding.

Why should I feel discouraged?
Why should the shadows come?
Why should my heart be lonely
And long for heaven and home?

When Jesus is my portion,
My constant friend is he.
His eye is on the sparrow
And I know he watches me.

Regardless of the pain we feel at the loss of a loved one, regardless of the anger and fear when someone betrays a trust, we must remember that God does indeed watch over us all. Things are not what they seem. The faithful will always overcome any and all obstacles in their paths in the end. Why? Because God, our Creator, promised it would be so, and Jesus, our Savior, died so that it would be so. Death is not an ending but a beginning. The cross does not stand for suffering and pain but for life, a life in Christ sustained by a deep and steadfast faith, a faith that "moves mountains" and turns the darkest of days into a day of rejoicing.

I sing because I'm happy.
I sing because I'm free.
For his eye is on the sparrow
And I know he watches me.

He watches me and you. All of God's creation is under God's loving care. For we have been promised the same victory over death that Christ was promised as long as we believe and persevere in our faith.

It is this faith that enabled our ancestors to withstand the long, hot days of cruel, seemingly endless labor; it is this faith that brought so many to these shores to begin a new life and enabled them to rebuild those lives after years of war, poverty, tragedy, poor education, and despair. It was this faith that caused our brothers and sisters in Christ to dance and sing of their joy and love of Jesus Christ.

They were indeed happy and so indeed should we be if we share that same faith in a wonder-working God, a take-charge God, a righteous God, a liberating God, a God who makes a way out of no way.

> *Nobody knows the trouble I've seen,*
> *Nobody knows my sorrow.*
> *Nobody knows the trouble I've seen,*
> *Glory! Alleluia!*

How did they do it? How could they sing of trouble that is unparalleled and pervasive yet conclude with praise and thanksgiving? How, but through faith, an undying, unbeatable faith? Jesus died on the cross and was laid to rest in a donated tomb. His followers walked away in grief and sorrow.

But we know the rest of the story! We know that Jesus rose again on the third day, that the stone was rolled away and he walked out in resurrected glory. Glory! Alleluia! He went before those who continued to believe in him into Galilee where he commissioned them to spread the Good News of God's coming throughout the world for all of time. He then returned to his Father as we too shall one day return to the Father and Mother of us all.

Glory! Alleluia!

Turn away from fear. Turn away from anger and violence. Look for and find the face of Jesus shining out of each and every person that you meet, whoever and wherever they may be. Like you, they too are struggling with their faith. Believe in Jesus and be fulfilled! He is not dead! There is joy, great joy, to come if we only believe and live our lives in accordance with that belief.

Glory! Alleluia!

SOURCES OF SONG LYRICS

Songs are listed by their title or commonly known first name in the order in which they are used in the text:

- I Couldn't Hear Nobody Pray (Spiritual)

- I've Been 'buked (Spiritual)

- Were You There? (Spiritual)

- The Lord Is My Light and My Salvation (Psalm)

- Lord, Help Me to Hold Out (James Cleveland © Planemar Music 1974)

- The Virgin Mary Had a Baby Boy (Spiritual)

- Give Me Jesus (Spiritual)

- Sweet Little Jesus Boy (Robert McGimsey)

- Amazing Grace (John Newton, 1725–1807)

- There Is a Balm in Gilead (Spiritual)

- We've Come This Far by Faith (Albert A. Goodson © Manna Music 1963)

- Sinner, Please Don't Let This Harvest Pass (Spiritual)

- Hush, Hush, Somebody's Calling My Name (Spiritual)

- Sometimes I Feel Like a Motherless Child (Spiritual)

- Pass Me Not, Oh Gentle Savior (Fanny Crosby, 1820–1915)

- Honor, Honor unto the Dying Lamb

- His Eye Is on the Sparrow (Civilla Martin/Charles Gabriel)

- Nobody Knows the Trouble I've Seen (Spiritual)